Time and Life Cycles

The spirit's journey through time

Elizabeth Diane

Preface to the 2019 Edition

This booklet is a quick overview of original ideas that have endured, a true description of unconscious responses as observed and studied between 1997 and 2011. It is an on-the-spot record of my actual responses and feelings. In the way a technician observes reactions in a lab experiment, I was recording thought mechanisms built in my nature. I was watching my deepest heart in action, the first description of the very fibers of what I am. This study enabled me to fully recover my natural self in an age of computers and the virtual reality. I found a greater capacity to be truly human.

After organizing the information for the 2012 publication, I continued to test and share the system that represents a natural phenomenon. . In 2018, the piles of work took on a reasonable form and I published *"The Heart's Mind: How unconscious responses in life and work naturally improve our lives while we make other plans."* It is a readable history about the discovery of what I came to call *The Cycle of Unconscious Response*™ and this booklet serves as a supplement to that story.

I treasure the original record because what happened at the beginning can never occur in that way ever again. I offer this work for the benefit of others who seek greater understanding through observing nature. In this case, we may begin to grasp the essence of our own human nature.

Elizabeth Diane

Changes to the 2012 original:

In the "Days of the Month" section:

- To emphasize the meaning of numbers for the 12 phases of *The Cycle of Unconscious Response™* repetitive descriptions for every day of the month were deleted.

- Keywords that are currently used for each phase were added, the first word is for the principle operating in the phase; the second word is for the natural response during the phase. For example, the original read as, "1 – One" and the new version reads as, "Day 1 – One: Impact/Intuition."

- A table for thirty-one days was added to illustrate the days of the month and how they conform to the principles of *The Cycle of Unconscious Response™*.

- One semantic adjustment was made is to replace the term "righteous authority" (referring to the power of love) with the term, "authority of the new good."

Other notes:

The diagrams remain as they appeared in the 2012 original.

The term "Time and Life Cycles™" now carries the trademark symbol.

Time and Life Cycles

The spirit's journey through time

"The Lord is not slack concerning his promise..."

There is a flow to life, just as there is a flow to water, air and nature. Growth has a pattern that repeats, a created order that produces life.

This interpretation of patterns and cycles I observed in time and life suggests that there is an order beneath the things in life we cannot escape. Change, confusion and adjustment are common in current times. Yet, we intuitively know there is something that keeps us from utter chaos.

If God is love, then the Universe will demonstrate it. Religion is useless now, if it cannot teach how love works. Love is essential to life, and the numbers demonstrate a logic built into God's creation. It shows that the Universe moves forward in time, always positive, always reassuring. It is love, in fact.

A calculable and measurable unfolding of time occurs around us, as regular as the ticking of a clock and as steady as the passing months. This is a timeless system that lies beneath all that we see. Its patterns are repetitive and observable. It is a life support system that we subconsciously rely on.

This is not special revelation, nor is it a new faith. I am reporting on phenomena I observed and recorded over several years' time, between 1997 and 2011 — cycles of time, and of patterns of our subconscious life that coincide with time. It is sometimes difficult to see the goodness that I now believe life manufactures as consistently as an apple tree manufactures leaves and fruit. These observations and studies have convinced me that Love is built into every molecule of the Universe. I hope this little book helps you to see it, too.

Elizabeth

Introduction

In history past, when ships crossed the ocean, they struggled against tides and currents, sometimes finding themselves going backwards. Then the ocean currents were discovered, revealing virtual conveyor belts going various directions through the waters. The navigators plotted a course so that the ship took the "path" heading in the desired direction. Problem solved.

At our core, we are spiritual beings in a flesh-and-blood body. We intuitively move in "paths" that have direction and reasonable order. We experience goodness in life, but accidentally, if we judge by what we see externally. We can also see with our spiritual "eyes" the place where goodness resides with regularity, much like those paths in the oceans.

The *Time and Life Cycles*™ are an expression of observable repetitive patterns, perceived by the subconscious. Just as the deep ocean currents cannot be seen on the surface, in the depths of the subconscious, there are "currents" that guide us safely through time.

If this is an actual phenomenon, as described here, others should be able to observe it, study it, and verify its nature. If you agree that the core of a human is spirit, an entity that lives beyond the death of the body, you may be able to verify the existence of the world where our spirit-self lives free.

WINTER

Before the year begins: Zero

Before life begins, there is a hovering ... a pause ... a building up of invisible energy. Looking on the surface, there is no sign of *life*. Then comes the moment when that invisible energy touches matter of its own kind, deep within the human heart.

January

Deep within a person lies a force, asleep — or so it would seem. Nonexistent, certainly *immaterial*, to the material world. When *energy* makes contact in a human being, a latent force is ignited. This is the beginning of life, the power of activity.

Even the subconscious waits, unaware that it will soon translate this new thing into messages the mind can perceive. Certainly, there is no evidence in the body of the arrival of new power. Yet, it is vibrant and active, in constant motion. In the depths of a person, this vibrancy has a profound effect. The nature of life is to grow and expand.

A snap electrifies the body's motor responses. A tremor runs through the path that leads to the surface and out to the material world. There is no doubt energy has bonded with matter.

The subconscious is awakened and is introduced to a concept. A hope has arrived, and the body is moved by the intangible heart. A desire forms, one without an intellectual expression. There is no explanation, no defense for what moves the body toward this new desire. It is spiritual, not material. Nothing in reality is compatible or cooperative with this superior energy.

It is strange to the tangible world, yet the new form of energy fits comfortably, naturally, in the spirit-being that lives inside the body. There, we accept any trace of life; it *is in our nature* to respond. We *know* this reality, against all reason. Everything in our being leans toward it and drinks it in like cool water.

The tremor — the electricity of it — affects us from deep within and startles our minds. It brings chaos to the soul. The mind is caught off guard, the body loses its repose, the tongue throws words at random, hoping to make sense of the thing. We have nothing worked out to translate the impact into rational behavior.

Intellect momentarily becomes docile. Natural desire and purpose fail to control the body. The heart is freed from the grip of mind and body. The power of life, pure and simple, overcomes matter. There is a glow and intensity that reality lacks, in its absence. The unity of spirit and matter is real; we don't yet understand it.

February

Gradually, and with determination, the mind recovers. Survival depends on capturing and subduing this "extranatural" invasion. The mind overrides emotion with logic. Still, the reasoning is subjective, unique to each individual, and then it is sequential and orderly.

Our mind evaluates the new arrival, observes the natural intuitive reaction of the body, judges it, and weaves the whole experience inside of reason. Calm returns with the power to control and the assurance of survival. In the subconscious, the new is quickly sorted into existing priorities. It is a unique and subjective survival pattern, built gradually through responses to similar events over time, even from childhood.

March

Reality challenges our complacency. Facts confront what we thought was victory over the new and submission to our "truth." The nature of this living force is that it cannot be stopped. At the arrival of a new, living and motivating concept, an attitude is changed in the subconscious — at our core — and life shifts around it. Reality forces us to defend our subconscious decisions, our truth.

Ultimately, we must choose a position with regard to others. Living out a subconscious decision will always bring encounters with others. Immediately, depending on our internal compass, we confront, avoid or cooperate with others who have their own priorities and purposes. We must make choices when paths cross. Until we take a position, we cannot truly live.

SPRING

April

Once deeper decisions are made, new life begins to appear on the surface. As routines resume, we work with the modified internal compass. We navigate around people and situations according to our subtle adjustments. Our activity, and the conversations that flow around us, reflect our response to the new concept.

The core purpose holds, and we work out the details to stay on top, to survive. As we walk out, externally, the change that took place internally, we become confident again that the body still represents our rational selves. The external has credibility, more than the internal self.

Through trial and error we find that we make better progress with our own priorities if we make room for others to progress in theirs. We balance asserting our will with allowing others to assert theirs. In doing so, we develop mutual cooperation and mutual benefit. If there is conflict, it stems from the imbalance of one having advantage, or forcing advantage, over another. Life supports cooperation and respect.

May

When the new becomes a natural part of our previous routine, we lose track of it and it loses its strangeness. Things are not the same as before, however. Life is vibrant. A new quality and ability has been added to our inner person. It has been strengthened, and the impact of new life finds its way to the surface.

Often, there is a burst of energy that announces the change, like a flower in spring. It is a realization of the *fact* of internal change. It is so real, we may think that dreams have become reality. It is real, but it is the promise of fruit, just as a flower is. Just as the flower falls away, the blush of success seems to vanish. But the promise is real, and the fruit will follow.

June

A person becomes vigorous, at this point. Just how the new strength and vigor came about is forgotten. There is a quickening, a fusion of heart and mind, of body and soul. Every human ability seems to come forward, at last. There is an ease to the power, a charisma that attracts and enlivens others. It appears that success has finally come; reward for the hard labor. Obstacles move aside, it seems. The dream has made an appearance as fact, as a result of our strength, our work.

Success is a product of the world in balance. A world in balance requires equality of material and spiritual. So, just when success seems within our grasp, just before the crown is placed on the proud brow — our power system stalls and the whole thing starts to unravel. As the vision slips away, frustration turns to acceptance. After all, to succeed so easily would be unnatural — or supernatural. We intuitively understand that the nature of life includes imperfection.

Yet, we did, in fact, touch the new heights we

reached for. We momentarily broke the spell of the ordinary. Hope burns brighter in the wreckage. *Next time*, we say to ourselves. *Next time...*

SUMMER

July

Empowered by success, again we throw ourselves into the fray. But now it's as if the power we just experienced was an illusion. Now what usually works for us has no effect, as if our hands are tied. Nothing responds the way we expect it to. The limitation of our strengths and gifts becomes painfully clear.

At times like this, we can see that life goes on, making progress that we can't take credit for. So success *isn't* only a product of our labor. Life, it seems, has a power of its own, accomplishing some of our work, benefiting us for its own mysterious reasons. We pocket these rewards like a ten-dollar bill found on the sidewalk.

August

Nature gives us trees and fruit; we can only tend them and harvest the crop. It makes one wonder

about life and the reasons behind having to work...
But never mind. Reality resumes its pace, we recover
our strength and set to the work again. This time, our
effort is tempered with humility, forced to accept the
reality that we can never make life perfect. Our
subconscious already knows this.

Subconsciously, it adds up. I do all I can to
thrive in an environment that is built to oppose me.
Yet, all that I accomplish has no value beyond the
material. Deep within me, I am most satisfied with
the by-product of the struggle: the activity of life
itself, personal accomplishment, love. Many things in
life whet our appetites for more.

Anticipation begins to build; for what, I cannot
tell. I shift, I feel pressure. I'm a little frustrated
because nothing is clear, except the feeling that I'm
about to experience something new. I am moving
away from something, toward something else. Maybe
it's a break in this long-building tension; I just can't
see to the other side.

September

Hope breaks through, and a kindling of love. I feel growth and expansion. Slowly, something begins to emerge. New, unique life. I am distracted by pain. It is tearing me away from the place where I used to be. It feels like a death, but I begin to see/feel a thing take shape — something I have hoped and longed for. It is familiar, and yet there has never been anything like it in my life before.

[The universe whispers: "Love conquers all"]

The life force that intruded and forced me to adapt and change all year was a connection between spirit and matter within me. Love was its intention all along. I am overwhelmed by incredulous joy. My heart knows what my mind barely imagined, and what my voice cannot speak. This is the realization of hope, yet all the struggle neutralizes my elation. This is, after all, "normal."

AUTUMN

October

After its arrival, love loses its unearthly, heavenly quality. Reality grows over it like a fungus, obscuring its brilliance. We inventory its strengths and weaknesses and go to work, fitting it in, dressing it up, shifting around it. Thoughts turn it over in our minds, judging its quality. *Will it survive in reality*?

I am of one kind; it is another. The discrepancy between the two becomes acute. I must adapt, if I am to keep the bit of new ground given to me. I become so engrossed in what change requires of me that I feel vulnerable to life's callous and aged road. In spite of the realities, I somehow manage to fit neatly, increasingly more fluidly in the stream. As I change, I get stronger.

November

Ambiguity is the enemy.

Survival requires that we have no regret, that we let go of the old and embrace the new. There's no denying that reality has been changed by this new conceptual, intangible reality. Whatever life was before its appearance is over now. Wistfully, we watch the old wither away as a fledgling goodness takes its place.

There is no stopping change, and it will not be moved from its place. The old becomes history, the new takes root, one of many seeds of change. The change is always good, in the end. Love, indeed, conquers all, moving constantly forward, inch by heartfelt inch.

December

By now, the journey of transformation seems slight and inconsequential, the long series of changes are over. A new love, now, is a natural and common occurrence; so common, that if we judge it by reasoning, it fades into the background, overwhelmed by the natural senses. It is in a flash of insight, or in a loving touch, that a heart is made tender, and we perceive love's true power above the transient events of a short lifetime on the planet.

The sum of our reflection on the year is this: We survived.

End of the Year: At Zero Again

Before life begins, there is a hovering … a pause … a building up of invisible energy. Looking on the surface, there is no sign of **life**. Then comes the moment when that invisible energy touches matter of its own kind, deep within the human heart.

January

Deep within a person lies a force, asleep — or so it would seem...

Time and Life Cycles™ Numbers: One through Thirty-One

The Days of the Month:

An interpreted observation

(Original: June 23, 2003. Revisions: April 2008, June 2011)

Introduction

In science we learn that numbers are symbols of a universal language. Numbers have no doctrine and can be used to prove or disprove theories.

Time itself is measured in numbers applied to minutes, hours, days, weeks, months and years. It is not the clock or the calendar that sets time, rather, it is nature—the world in which we are placed. The *Time and Life Cycles*™ theory is rooted in a pattern of twelve.

This theory is not a matter of prophecy or faith, but rather a grid—a tool—a way to see what is happening beyond and beneath the physical. It can be verified independently by observing and understanding one's own internal thoughts.

The meanings of some numbers are taken from the Bible. For example, the number three is associated with the Godhead: Father, Son, and Holy Spirit, and indicates relationship. The seventh day is the number for rest, after six days of work.

The best illustration of love overcoming oppression is in the story of the Israelites' exodus from Egypt. Ten plagues loosened the Pharaoh's power over them. It was the undoing of slavery, one step at a time. I interpret the number eleven as disintegration of natural power, and the system that enables slavery. Twelve, then, refers to the resulting freedom, and a foundation of righteous authority that replaced slavery. The only righteous authority is love.

Although this system is based on numbers, it is neither scientific nor complete. If my observations do not bear out to be true over much time, independently verified by others, they are false. I offer this record of my observations so that they can be verified, contradicted, amplified, and modified by the observations of others until the truth is more accurately reflected in the conclusions.

Days of the Month

One to thirty-one is the longest sequence in the way we count time by months. We will look at the meaning of each day, implied by each of the 12 principles.

Days one through twelve are the first level, days 13 through 24, the second level; and days 24 through 31, partially complete a third level.

Day 1 – One: Impact/Intuition

Beginning; being there and experiencing a new thing; not understanding; react intuitively and instinctively, from the heart, often with emotion.

Day 2 – Two: Recovery/Priorities

Understanding; reason returns; understand what you just experienced; regain perspective and a sense of priorities.

Day 3 – Three: Position/Relate

Relate to the people associated with the new;

relationships are formed; choose to accept or reject; take a position.

Day 4 – Four: Path/Determination

Walk out the choice; move on with addition of new experience, resuming previous routine.

Day 5 – Five: Harmony/Assimilation

Assimilation; the new becomes integrated with what was before. This is a process that cannot be observed; assimilation is a blending, a marrying into one.

Day 6 – Six: Strength/Breakthrough

Having assimilated the new, acting in our own strength; six is the sum of human strength, and its limitation; results may or may not be to our liking.

Day 7 – Seven: Meaning/Perspective

Our strengths are restrained, ineffective; we see what is accomplished without our work and strength of our will.

Day 8 – Eight: Transition/Preparation

Begin again; new beginnings; starting again after rest; moving, with the effects of one through seven, into position for what's to come.

Day 9 – Nine: Manifestation/Visible Unity

Bringing forth a new thing, as giving birth; being delivered and/or delivering; includes equal parts pain and joy.

Day 10 – Ten: Comprehension/Judgment

Assess what was brought forth; judgment; the event that illustrates the sum of choices at stages one through nine.

In one sense, ten is the number of human authority, whose power is judgment. In another sense, it is the number of the judgment on an authority structure that is natural and imperfect.

Day 11 – Eleven: Emergence/Letting Go

Disintegration; dismantling of the natural structure that kept us in place until love's perfect way is given, the system of good that cannot be violated forever.

Day 12 – Twelve: Permanence/Acceptance

Right authority is established in the current concern of the heart. This authority may not have any tangible form whatever, but is the natural, inviolable system that will begin to produce goodness.

The universal system of right authority can neither be resisted nor ignored. The only righteous authority is love. When righteous, loving authority is established in an area of the heart, we are healed.

Heart (spirit, breath, life) change is internal, but has an effect on our minds, emotions and bodies. We begin to live differently in the world in that area of concern.

Days of the Month, Arranged by the 12 Phases of *The Cycle of Unconscious Response*™

Phases One through Six

Principle:	Impact	Recovery	Position	Path	Harmony	Strength
	Phase One	Phase Two	Phase Three	Phase Four	Phase Five	Phase Six
1st cycle	1	2	3	4	5	6
2nd cycle	13	14	15	16	17	18
3rd cycle	25	26	27	28	29	30

Phases Seven through Twelve

Principle:	Meaning	Transition	Manifestation	Comprehension	Emergence	Permanence
	Phase Seven	Phase Eight	Phase Nine	Phase Ten	Phase Eleven	Phase Twelve
1st cycle	7	8	9	10	11	12
2nd cycle	19	20	21	22	23	24
3rd cycle	31					

Hindsight: Using 20/20 Vision

Time and Life Cycles™:
Tools to see your own path

Pattern, not Prophecy

How does someone "see" what isn't there?

An important first step is to realize that every person consists of heart, soul, mind, and body. We generally accept this four-part description as the sum of our complexity. We think with our minds, we feel with our hearts, our bodies connect with all material things. When we get to "soul," we turn that over to theologians to define for us.

Some time in the 1980's, I wondered what was meant by the idea that the word of God can even divide soul and spirit. Since religion seems to equate the two and offered no real explanation, I studied to understand the difference between soul and spirit.

These are my conclusions: "Soul" is rooted in life on the planet, and is the internal experience of will and emotion; it is our temporal personality. Conversely, "spirit" is rooted in eternity, and does not depend on information from our short earthly experience. The spirit's "intuition" is based in timeless truth, and so, is a more powerful influence on our lives, over the long term.

The goal of the *Time and Life Cycles*™ is to provide a way to use our minds to separate actions motivated by the soul from actions motivated by the spirit. What I found is that the choices of the spirit are more solid and fruitful than the choices of the soul.

One way of seeing the choices of your spirit is to look back over some of your life history. The will- and emotion-based activity falls away, and, if my observations are correct, the sequence in your history that matches the sequence of the *Time and Life Cycles*™ is the journey of your spirit through time.

On the next pages are:

1) A diagram of the *Time and Life Cycles*™ in the form of a clock, showing the sequence of months as the numbers.

2) A similar diagram showing the first twelve years of the 21st Century, which is also the third millennium from the birth of Christ.

3) A form showing the human life span in

phases of the *Time and Life Cycles*™, with another form with space for you to make notes from your reflections on your life.

The only way to test this theory is to look back at your personal history and your internal experience to engage the useful 20/20 hindsight. If you are affected in your spirit by this information, it will draw you back; otherwise it will have no meaning for you.

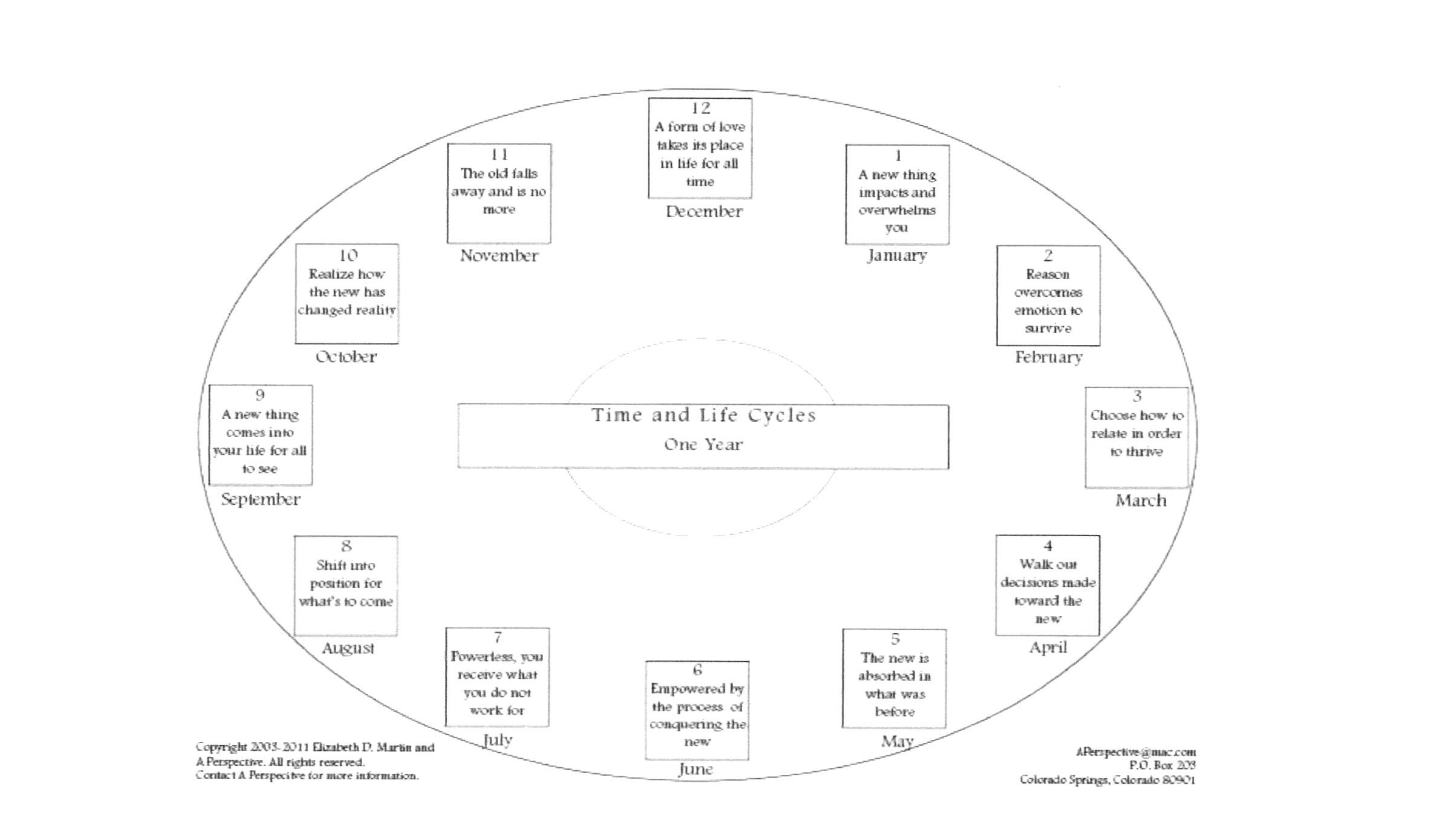

APerspective@mac.com
P.O. Box 203
Colorado Springs, Colorado 80901

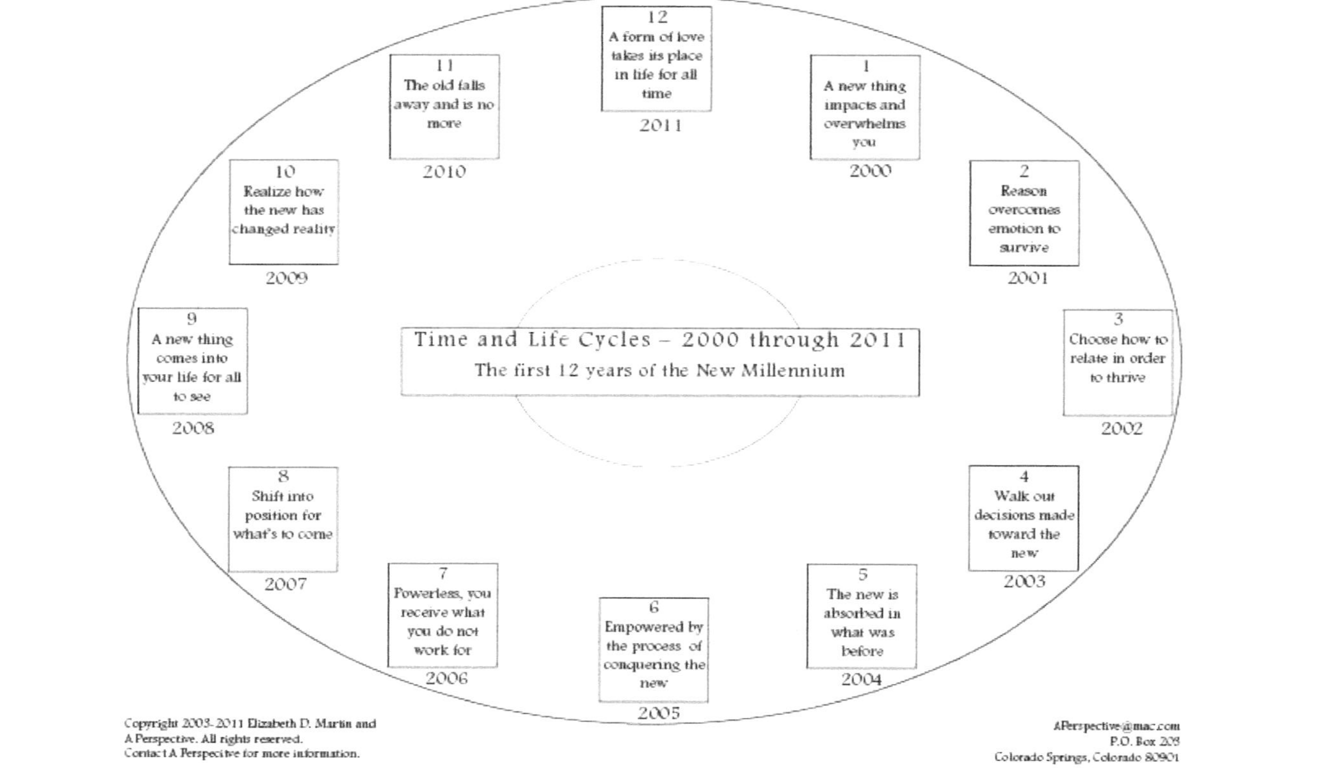

APerspective@mac.com
P.O. Box 208
Colorado Springs, Colorado 80901

The ultimate "Big Picture": Phases of a Lifespan and the eventual exit from time to eternity

PHASE ONE
Age 0-12

Love brings us to earth; we see, we learn and we adapt. Our choices are made from a basic, intuitive nature, abilities we bring with us from the womb.

PHASE TWO
Age 13-24

Intuitively we realize the full impact of living in the world. During this phase, we construct a personal priority system and value structure. It is an "I" position as separate from others.

PHASE THREE
Age 25-36

Take a position toward life, in terms of how we relate to others. Our decisions have to do with how our values and priorities differ from that of others; an idenity.

PHASE FOUR
Age 37-48

We walk out the choices we made about how we want life to conform to our values. We navigate through conversations and events to anchor our distinct place in the world.

PHASE FIVE
Age 49-60

Having established a place externally, all that we have experienced blends together and we feel complete within ourselves; mature. It is the height of personal confidence.

PHASE SIX
Age 61-72

The time of our greatest human strength—and its limitation. In full maturity we can function according to our the abilities and are able to fulfill the work we were born to do while in the body.

PHASE Seven
Age 73-84

Our bodies being weakened, our hearts are strengthened as we see the greater and truer meaning of life relative to the physical.

PHASE EIGHT
Age 85-96

We shift into change, caught between two worlds—the material and the spiritual—and we live both at once.

PHASE NINE
Age 97-108

A new birth as the spirit self rises above the material self and internally comes into the eternal space.

PHASE TEN
Age 109-120

Full realization of completion as the spirit self looks out into the world.

PHASE ELEVEN
DEATH

Time vanishes as we let go of the body.

PHASE TWELVE
ETERNITY

Love wins.

The ultimate "Big Picture": Phases of a human life span and the eventual exit from time to eternity.

Phase 1:	Phase 2:	Phase 3	Phase 4	Phase 5	Phase 6	Phase 7:	Phase 8	Phase 9	Phase 10:	Phase 11	Phase 12
Age 0-12	Age 13-24	Age 25-36	Age 37-48	Age 49-60	Age 61-72	Age 73-84	Age 85-96	Age 97-108	Age 109-120	Death	Eternity
Love brings us to earth; we see, we learn and we adapt.	We realize the full impact of life on the planet.	We decide our position, as we relate to others.	We walk out the choices we made.	We become one within ourselves.	The time of our greatest human strength and its limitation.	We see what works in spite of our weakness.	We shift into change, caught between two worlds.	Our internal self makes it to the external.	Full realization of a spirit self.	Time vanishes	Love wins

How would you characterize each phase of your life?

Age 0-12	Age 13-24	Age 25-36	Age 37-48	Age 49-60	Age 61-72	Age 73-84	Age 85-96	Age 97-108	Age 109-120	Can you see it?
										Note attitudes or circumstances that characterize your life toward the end of phases you have passed. Compare your view with the Phase description. It takes time for your mind to become aware of subconscious patterns in your life. Use this chart as a tool to reflect on the meaning of your life. Our decisions either put us in harmony with it, or at odds. It doesn't matter; Love wins, either way.

NOTES